THE KENNEL CLUB

MAN'S BEST FRIEND

An Illustrated History of Our Relationship with Dogs

WILDFIRE

CONTENTS

A 1930s European postcard featuring a Smooth-haired Dachshund. Known in Germany as the Teckel (badger dog), these little sausage dogs are renowned for being intelligent, lively and courageous to the point of rashness.

CLARE BALDING CBE

Every page of this book makes me smile, as the photos show us with crystal clarity the deep bond between humans and their dogs. There is love and pride in every picture, and it is a visual record of the diversification of breeds kept in the UK and beyond. It also shows us the way in which dogs have become not just domesticated but integrated into the family over the centuries.

There are so many highlights but I had to laugh at the picture of the father and his newborn baby in the 'Love Me, Love My Dog' chapter, as he clearly chose to place the dog rather than his child in the centre of the shot. Then there are the wonderful compositions that prove my theory that dogs make far better photographic subjects than people. My personal favourite is the three English Springer Spaniel puppies spilling out of the Birmingham trophy from 1934 (see the 'Puppy Love' chapter opener).

Every photo shows a different role a dog can play or a different job it can do. Whether they're acting as playmate and guardian of children, advertising model, propaganda tool, co-driver, warm and loving companion, herder of sheep, catcher of vermin, brave and loyal soldier or champion show dog, they could and can do it all. This book is a unique visual celebration of the many ways in which dogs enhance our lives.

Heidi Hudson, as the curator of the Kennel Club's photographic collection, has been the inspiration behind this fantastic anthology. This book is the product of years spent scouring the internet for rare or unusual snaps that capture the history of our life with our canine companions. This book is a testament to her expertise and the treasured heritage of The Kennel Club, as well as providing a wonderful pictorial catalogue of our deep and lasting friendship with dogs.

INTRODUCTION

The relationship between mankind and dogs has a long and remarkable history, going back thousands of years and leaving an indelible mark on both species. Originally valued primarily as hunting companions, dogs helped humans track and capture prey, then later, as early civilisations emerged, they found roles guarding settlements and protecting livestock. As dogs became more domesticated, the bond between canines and humans grew ever stronger, but throughout most of history only the very wealthiest people kept them solely as pets.

It was not until the early nineteenth century that people began to think differently about their canine friends. The industrial and agricultural revolutions changed the way people worked and animal labour was no longer so necessary. The British public also began to be concerned with animal welfare and laws were passed forbidding cruelty to dogs and other creatures. At the same time, more people had the leisure and money to keep dogs as pets and companions, rather than as working animals.

Perhaps it is unsurprising, then, that around this time a new trend started to emerge: competitive dog shows. Early shows took place in pubs, at agricultural fairs and in private homes. Over time, these became formal competitions, and all the major cities held their own dog shows in grand venues.

Meanwhile, in the countryside, the landed gentry began to develop a new activity of their own. Field trials were a formal test of skill for working gundogs who assisted the sporting shooter. Unlike dog showing, which attracted a wide range of participants and spectators from all classes, this was an elite sport for the upper classes only.

In response to these innovations, The Kennel Club was founded in 1873 by Mr Sewallis Evelyn Shirley and twelve other men. The founders wanted to have a consistent set of rules for governing these popular new activities of dog showing and field trials, and to ensure that they were run fairly and with the welfare of the dogs in mind. It was the first national kennel club in the world.

At that time, dogs were given generic pet names like Dash and Shep. It could be hard to tell individual dogs apart, so, in 1880, The Kennel Club started a registrations system. All dogs were given a unique name and a record was kept of their parentage for several generations – what we now call a pedigree.

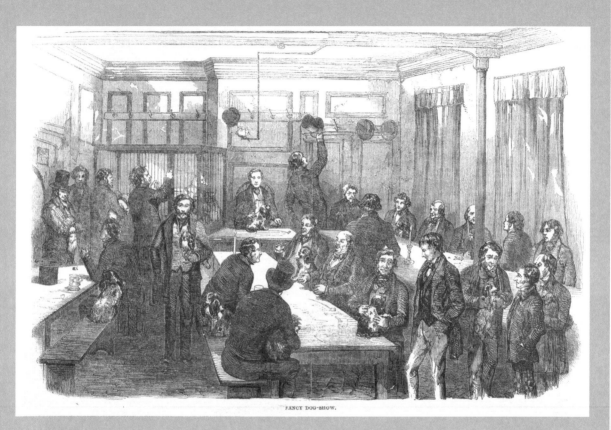

FANCY DOG-SHOW.

Previous spread: A famous image from 1949 showing a young boy and his dog looking at posters outside the show at Olympia (in those days Crufts still had an apostrophe!).

This page: An early dog show in The Eight Bells pub in Westminster, London, 1851.

Charles Cruft, his personal secretary, and Crufts show manager Mr Robert Keddell reviewing photographs from Crufts, date unknown.

Dog shows continued to go from strength to strength in the late Victorian period, becoming popular as a day out for both spectators and participants. Unusually for the time, it was seen as a suitable pursuit for all ages and backgrounds; men and women of all social classes could compete on an equal footing. The most famous of these shows was Crufts, founded by entrepreneur Charles Cruft in 1891, which is now The Kennel Club's own world-famous flagship event.

Today, The Kennel Club's purpose is to make a positive difference for dogs and their owners. It is the largest organisation in the UK devoted to dog health, welfare and training. It still supports the dog showing and dog activities scene nationwide, as well as running the UK's largest registration database for pedigree dogs and a register for crossbreed dogs involved in competitive dog activities. It works with vets, researchers and animal welfare organisations to make a difference to dog health. And it gives information, advice and support to people who want to welcome a dog or puppy into their home. In 2023, it was granted a Royal Prefix to mark the 150th anniversary of The Kennel Club.

There is also another, lesser-known side of its work – which is where this book comes in. The Kennel Club Photographic Collection's remit is to collect photographic records and image history relating to dogs – and in particular the British pedigree dog.

Tucked away in the basement of its offices in Mayfair, London, The Kennel Club's collection holds an estimated two million images in all formats – some digital, but also encompassing prints, negatives, and historic early formats like rare glass plates, daguerreotypes, ambrotypes, tin types, glass plate slides, and magic mirror slides. It also holds postage stamps, cigarette cards, candy cards, calendars, advertisements and postcards featuring dogs. This book is only a small reflection of what it keeps in its collection.

These items have come to The Kennel Club in all sorts of ways over the years – by donation and legacies, specialist dealers, auctions, even lucky finds in charity shops and jumble sales. Many gaps remain, though, and it suffered a major loss of photographs and other records during the Second World War when The Kennel Club building sustained bomb damage.

The British monarchy has a long and loving association with dogs and some of the collection's best-loved photographs show members of the Royal Family with their favourite canine companions. We have included one of our favourites in this book – a *carte de visite* showing Alexandra, Princess of Wales, later Queen Alexandra (1844–1925), with one of her many dogs. Queen Alexandra was a knowledgeable and active member of the dog world and was the founding patron of the Ladies Kennel Association. She was a keen and talented photographer herself, often photographing her relatives with their dogs.

Another favourite included in this book is a recent photographic find, showing an English Toy Terrier wearing a cap and a custom-made jacket carrying the now defunct *Dog World* paper, which was one of the major weekly dog papers in the UK. The Kennel Club was fortunate to buy the entire *Dog World* photographic archive to preserve its legacy for future generations. We gained photographs of many famous dogs, previously unseen photos from Crufts and of course some rare images like this one.

We have also included a very rare photogravure – a combination of an early photograph and engraving – of a Gordon Setter called Dandy, winner of the first formal dog show which took place in Newcastle-upon-Tyne in 1859. Plus of course there are dozens of other favourites, chosen for their quirky character and to showcase the fun side of dog ownership.

Dog photographs are incredibly important. They are more than one moment in time captured on film or in digital form – they are visual historical records of the pedigree dog through the ages (and dogs in general). They are symbols of our affection towards our canine companions and provide lasting visual memories of our relationship with dogs. They are at times pieces of art. Without photographs, we would not be able to study how dogs have changed over the years or use this vital evidence to help improve their health and wellbeing. Lastly, dogs in photographs just make us smile and remind us how dogs are truly man's best friend.

Heidi Hudson,
Curator, Photographic Collections, The Kennel Club
Ciara Farrell,
Library and Collections Manager, The Kennel Club

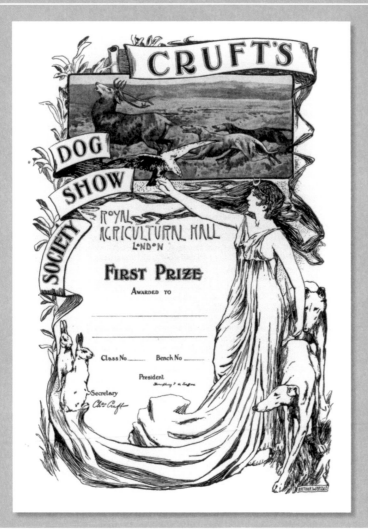

A Crufts winner's certificate from the 1880s.

CHAPTER 1

LOVE ME, LOVE MY DOG

Previous spread: A woman carrying her Samoyed into Crufts dog show at Islington Agricultural Hall, *c.* 1920s. Around this time, Charles Cruft eclipsed The Kennel Club's own show by continuing to add classes and special competitions, so that by 1925 the number of entries stood at 8,008, with exhibitors including King George V.

This page: An upper-class Victorian lady posing with her two dogs – a Spitz breed type and a Yorkshire Terrier breed type on her lap. This photo was taken in a studio on Regent Street, London, in the 1860s.

A *carte de visite* (*c.* 1870s) featuring a Victorian woman outside her house with a crossbreed dog. *Cartes de visite* – 'visiting cards' – were commonly traded among friends and acquaintances from the 1860s onwards, and albums of the cards were displayed in Victorian parlours.

A dashing young London gentleman poses with his Fox Terrier on this *carte de visite* from the late 1860s. Fox Terriers were a new breed at the time, the official pedigree dating from 1870. Most modern strains of white Terriers are descended from just three dogs: Old Jock, Trap and Tartar.

Another *carte de visite* from the 1870s, showing a wealthy-looking gentleman posing with his Labrador crossbreed. The photographer has managed to get the dog to look directly at his camera lens, with ears alert!

H. Walters

117, CROWN STREET,
IPSWICH.

A cabinet card from the 1880s featuring a young father proudly showing off his toddler and his Terrier crossbreed. Cabinet cards were larger than *cartes de visite*, and consisted of photographs mounted on thin cardboard backing. They were often used to advertise photographers' services.

W. & D. DOWNEY,   **MISS AMY WILLIAMSON.**   61 EBURY ST., LONDON, W.

Reproduced by Permission from Original Negative.

THE PHOTOGLYPTIC CO.   EDINBURGH.

The popular actress Miss Amy Williamson is captured on camera alongside her black Poodle or Portuguese Water Dog early breed type. This reproduction cabinet card was commercially available throughout the UK and Europe in the 1880s.

Disdéri & Cº. *(Limited)*

H.R.H THE PRINCESS OF WALES

This *carte de visite* reproduction shows the Princess of Wales – later Queen Alexandra – with one of her companion dogs, possibly a Tibetan Terrier breed type. The photo was taken in November 1866 by the French photographer Disdéri.

STEREOSCOPIC COY.

Copyright

A *carte de visite* stereoscopic copy from the 1880s showing Queen Victoria with one of her Scotch Collies. The Queen was an avid dog-lover, owning over 620 canine pets in her lifetime.

The word 'stereoscopic' refers to the practice of two photographs being taken a few centimetres apart, roughly the distance between a human's eyes. When the two photos were viewed side by side through a special device, the brain would combine the two images, creating a three-dimensional sense of depth.

JOHN HART

179 & 181
CITY ROAD, E.C.

275
LEYTONSTONE ROAD E.

A cabinet card from the 1880s featuring a man showing off his racing Greyhound in the East End of London.

A young girl and her Rough Collie pose on a typical British street in this postcard from 1908.

A pre-First World War (c. 1904–1907) postcard featuring an elegant Edwardian lady holding her Maltese dog. It was stamped from Paris, France, and sent to a young man named Ralph Wade Esq. in Hampton Wick, Surrey. Little white companion dogs were a particular favourite of the upper classes at the time.

An Edwardian postcard (*c.* 1910s) featuring a little girl dressed in her Sunday best next to a Standard Poodle. It's likely the dog's owner was standing out of shot on the left to keep the dog still for the photograph. Poodles are one of our oldest breeds, dating back to the seventeenth century, and originally bred to retrieve waterfowl. The name comes from the German *pudel* or *pudelin*, which means to splash in the water.

This 1913 postcard features two Edwardian children with their Newfoundland crossbreed. Despite their size, Newfoundlands are known for their calm nature and gentle way with children – J. M. Barrie's Nana in *Peter Pan* was based on the author's own Newfoundland, Luath.

A small child stands next to a St Bernard breed type in a winter studio setting in this coloured postcard from the 1910s. St Bernards are another large breed famed for their sweet temperament.

LL. A.A. RR. Les Princes Léopold et Charles de Belgique.

Cliché Alexandre
BRUXELLES.

An Edwardian postcard
(*c.* 1909) featuring two
Belgian princes – Leopold
and Charles – with their dog,
either a Belgian Malinois
or German Shepherd Dog.
The older brother ruled as
Leopold III of Belgium but
he was later forced into exile
and eventually abdication.

A young Edwardian child from the 1910s holds the lead of his Schipperke, a breed believed to have originated in Belgium. The boy is wearing an Eton collar, a common style among British schoolboys at this time – not just those who attended Eton College.

FOR YOUR BIRTHDAY

This carries a message from doggie and me...
Our wishes both kind and sincere, ...
May joy be your guest on
this bright happy day,
And remain with
you all through
the year.

A colourised birthday
postcard from the Edwardian
era, depicting a young woman
and her Collie.

True Blue.

The stormy ocean roaring wide,
Between my love and me,
Can never, never yet divide
My heart and soul from thee.

Sentimental postcards for sailors away at sea became popular during the First World War. This one features a devoted lady with a Terrier crossbreed dog.

459 J ROTARY PHOTO. E.C. MISS GERTIE MILLAR. W & D. DOWNEY
LONDON. S.W COPYRIGHT

Thought this one would go with the other

A commercial postcard of the English actress Miss Gertie Millar with her Maltese breed type dog (*c.* 1920s). Millar was a popular star of musical comedies from her debut in 1892 at the age of thirteen until the end of the First World War.

The writing on the front reads: 'Thought this one would go with the other.' The card was not posted but it was addressed to a Miss Annie Pearse.

POLA NEGRI

An early 1920s postcard featuring the Polish actress Pola Negri with her Borzoi. Negri signed with Paramount Pictures in 1922, making her the first European actress in history to be contracted in Hollywood. Borzois were the favoured dog of the Russian Tsars and could only be gifted by the Russian royal family until they were all tragically killed during the revolution. It was no surprise that the Borzoi became a favoured breed for early Hollywood royalty as well.

A young woman in her seaside costume holds her Collie in a photographer's studio that has been styled to look like a beach. This black and white postcard from the 1920s has been partly colourised to give a more natural effect.

A press photo from Crufts 1966 showing a little boy and his two Fox Terriers, one real and one slightly less so!

Fox Terriers emerged in the 1860s, and by 1873 the Fox Terrier class at Birmingham Dog Show drew 276 entries. Three years later the Fox Terrier Club of England was formed and by the start of the twentieth century it was the most popular breed in England.

CHAPTER 2

PUPPY LOVE

J.H.COATH

666

SIX COASTGUARDS.

ROTARY PHOTO. E.C.

Previous spread: A press photo of English Springer Spaniel puppies in a Blackpool silver trophy cup from 1934, the year after the Blackpool Championship Dog Show was first held.

This page: A remarkably neat row of St Bernard puppies from a 1906 postcard. The national dog of Switzerland, the St Bernard is named after the monk who, in the eleventh century, founded a hospice to care for travellers on the perilous routes through the Alps. The breed is famous for its history of mountain rescues.

THE NEW ARRIVALS.

W.&K. 737.

An antiquarian postcard featuring four German Shepherd puppies, a breed that has gained worldwide popularity for its bravery and intelligence. They make excellent guard dogs and are often used for police work.

A vintage postcard featuring a Sealyham Terrier, Scottish Terrier and West Highland White Terrier. Terriers were originally bred to hunt vermin, often pursuing foxes, badgers and rats underground ('Terrier' comes from the Latin word *terra*, meaning earth). These brave and hardy game breeds have been popular in Britain for many centuries.

A handlebar-moustached Edwardian gentleman with his Smooth Fox Terrier and her three pups. One of the best examples of the breed was Donna Fortuna, bred in the 1890s by Francis Redmond, owner of the famous Totteridge Kennels and later chairman of The Kennel Club. Donna Fortuna's original show lead is preserved by The Kennel Club art collection.

THREE OF A KIND

R.P. 313

These adorable Labrador Retriever puppies demonstrate why the Labrador is the most popular of all pedigree breeds. Not only do they excel as service dogs, guide dogs and working gundogs, they also make great family pets.

LITTLE RASCALS

R.P. 341

Three Pekingese puppies poised for mischief – though they are in fact an aristocratic breed. 'Peke' types can be traced back to eighth-century China during the Tang dynasty, and became a favourite among the nobility in the Imperial Palace in Peking (now Beijing), hence the name.

A vintage Edwardian postcard of a little girl with a Terrier breed type puppy.

A personal album photo from the early 1900s, provenance unknown. The text on the back reads, 'This lady is my housekeeper. She is sometimes very grumpy, except on Monday mornings when she wants some money!' This formidable lady is seen here with her Terrier pup.

Just a line.

189

A vintage postcard of English Springer Spaniels, produced in 1930. The breed earned its name by its practice of 'springing' forward to flush game from undergrowth to be netted or shot.

An English Springer Spaniel mum proudly shows off her three puppies. Barrels and baskets are always a clever way to keep puppies in place while taking a family photo!

A vintage postcard showing six Rough Collie puppies sitting on a bench, clearly transfixed by something off-camera.

3. Cairn Terrier Puppies.

Photo by
Hugh Morton

The Cairn Terrier is perhaps best known as Toto from *The Wizard of Oz* – though it is actually a native Scottish breed. From the seventeenth century it was used in the Western Highlands and the Isle of Skye to keep down vermin.

CHAPTER 3

WORK LIKE A DOG

CHOCOLAT POULAIN

GOÛTEZ & COMPAREZ QUALITÉ SANS RIVALE

4 _ Ire Chien Munito.

Previous spread: Sled dogs in the Canadian Arctic on Dixon Island. Dogs have worked in the Arctic alongside humans for an incredible 17,000 years, most commonly the Siberian Husky, Alaskan Malamute, Samoyed, Canadian Eskimo Dog and Greenland Dog – all large, powerful breeds with thick coats and high endurance.

This page: A French chocolate bar trading card from France, *c.* 1880s. 'Le Chien Munito', owned by Signor Castelli from Italy, was a famous performing Poodle, who travelled throughout Europe entertaining the royals and celebrities of the day. This intelligent dog could supposedly play dominoes, do sums and spell using lettered cards.

A stereoview card from 1896 showing a Hound type breed pulling a milk cart. The use of dogs to deliver fresh milk was a common practice throughout Europe in the nineteenth century, particularly in Belgium, France and Germany.

J. J. - 8479. - Grand St-Bernard
Maître et Serviteurs

A Swiss postcard from the Hotel d'Angleterre in Vevey, Switzerland, in 1913, depicting two St Bernards with a Swiss monk. The breed was renowned for its Alpine rescue work, and during the First World War the dogs assisted the Red Cross and were used to carry supplies to troops in the Alps.

Campesino de Tenerife.

4146.

A vintage postcard from Tenerife, Spain, showing a farmer wearing his native costume, alongside a traditional Spanish working dog who would help with the cattle.

An Edwardian postcard photo *c.* 1915–1918 showing some gentlemen with their racing Whippets. Popular in northern England and Wales, Whippets were originally used to catch rabbits, and later trained to race by chasing lure or rags along alleyways. Nowadays this elegant dog is hugely popular as a show breed and as a gentle family pet.

An album photo from the 1930s, showing two French Hounds pulling a boulangerie and patisserie wagon in France. The seller is directing his cart with a dog on each side.

This vintage Belgian postcard from the 1920s shows a missionary and his loyal companion in the Arctic Circle.

PACK DOGS ON THE TRAIL
GROUSE MOUNTAIN VANCOUVER B. C.

A Canadian postcard from 1939 showing pack dogs in Vancouver. Working dogs were used to carry day packs for long treks through the wilderness with trappers or hunters. Dogs had to be fit and strong as well as having thick coats to protect them from the weather.

A PATHETIC MOURNER IN THE FUNERAL PROCESSION.

Cæsar, the Late King Edward's Favourite Dog.
"I BELONG TO THE KING."

With the Compliments of
SPRATT'S PATENT LIMITED

An advertising postcard for Spratt's dog food, *c.* 1915–1920. Caesar (1898–1914) was a Wire Fox Terrier who was the constant companion of King Edward VII. The dog had his own footman, slept next to the King's bed, and wore a collar that read: 'I am Caesar. I belong to the King.' After the King's death in 1910, Caesar walked in the funeral procession ahead of many leading heads of state.

A Belgian postcard from the 1930s showing a Congolese hunting party with their Basenjis – the only dog in the world that doesn't bark. The first Basenjis arrived in England in 1936 from central Africa, where they had been used as an all-purpose hunter working by sight and scent.

"TIM" GARDEN FETE 1928

This 1928 postcard shows 'Tim', a Terrier breed type, collecting for charity at a garden fete. Dogs were often used as fundraisers, collecting coins by having pouches or tin cans attached to their bodies with custom-made harnesses and costumes.

A rat catcher and his trusty ratter – a Sealyham Terrier. This Welsh breed takes its name from the village where it originated, in Pembrokeshire on the river Sealy. The village squire, Captain John Owen Edwardes, who developed the breed, lived in Sealyham Manor. Today the Sealyham Terrier is on the vulnerable native breed list due to its low numbers.

A press photo for the international sheepdog trials held in Hyde Park, London, in 1949. Mr Griff Pugh from Chester and his dog Sweep won third prize, Mr Tom Bonella of Kinross and his dog Glen came second, and the winner was Mr R. O. Williams with his dog Ben, from north Wales. All Border Collies, of course.

A 1949 press photo from Caledonian Kennels at Onibury, a village in Shropshire, showing how pups are turned into gundogs. Here some Labrador Retrievers and Cocker Spaniels are being trained in a 'sit' command as they watch some rabbits go past them.

A *Dog World* press photo from the 1940s. This English Toy Terrier is wearing a custom-made jacket carrying the now defunct *Dog World* paper, a weekly British newspaper that updated dog fanciers on the latest show results and news. English Toy Terriers are now one of our vulnerable native breeds.

A press photo from 1965 showing Mr J. Wylie with Mrs A. Watt's Cocker Spaniel Exton Monty, who won a diploma of merit in the Cocker Spaniel Championship that year.

9006   " SAY, PLEASE ! "   ROTARY PHOTO. E.C.

CHAPTER 4
BARKING MAD

Previous spread: An Edwardian postcard from 1906 depicting a Terrier and a Collie at afternoon tea. Photographers went to great lengths to pose dogs in anthropomorphic scenes, in order to cater for the tastes of the growing postcard market in the early twentieth century.

This page: This *carte de visite* reproduces the popular animal artist Edwin Landseer's famous painting, *Laying Down the Law* (1840). A satirical take on the legal profession, it depicts dogs in court with a French Poodle presiding as judge. The painting was inspired by a judge dining with Landseer, who commented that the Poodle belonging to the fashionable artist Count d'Orsay 'would make a capital Lord Chancellor'.

This Victorian glass plate slide (*c.* 1880s) may look like a bit of fun but it is actually a satirical comment on the politics of the day, aimed at the then Prime Minister. On the wall in the background you can just make out the phrases 'Why not tax cats', 'No muzzles' and – more controversially – 'No Gladstone'.

An antiquarian postcard (*c.* 1900s) depicting a variety of pedigree dogs enjoying a picnic. Poodles, Retrievers, Collies, Terriers and Schipperkes all feature in this jolly scene.

"NOW THEY'LL BLAME ME FOR THIS."

A leaky umbrella causes problems for the family pet in this Edwardian postcard from 1907.

Another humorous postcard from 1907, this is an art engraving turned into a postcard featuring a large Newfoundland breed type looking down on a small Black and Tan Terrier, the ancestor of the English Toy Terrier. In the US it became the Toy Manchester Terrier, pointing to its ancestry as the rat killer first developed during the Industrial Revolution.

The handwriting on the right reads: 'Jolly journey home pony's [*sic*] went well I did not walk far'.

CAMPING OUT.

Here's a jolly camping group —
Members of the dog-scout troop.

These Terrier type puppies enjoy a camping trip in this
pre-war postcard from 1912.

"LOVESICK"

A little boy offers his biscuit to his 'lovesick' Terrier type dog in this postcard from *c.* 1915.

ANIMAL STUDIES.
No. 13.

'A COLLIE'S INTEREST IN PICTURES".

LILYWHITE LTD.
ALL BRITISH PHOTO PRINTERS

A Rough Collie shows off its intelligence in this 1921 postcard. The founder of The Kennel Club, Mr S. E. Shirley, was a keen promoter of the Rough Collie, and Queen Victoria helped to popularise the breed when she brought some from Balmoral to her royal estates.

"Take my milk, madam, I'll wait."

A 1920s postcard showing a Yorkshire Terrier and his kitten friend. All modern-day Yorkies are thought to descend from a dog named Huddersfield Ben, born in 1865. It's believed that Scottish labourers brought their Terriers with them when they moved to Yorkshire to work in the mines and cotton mills, and this formed the basis of the breed.

"Oliver Twist."

A 1920s postcard depicting Bonzo the dog as Oliver Twist. Created by British artist George Studdy, Bonzo quickly became a phenomenon around the world, featuring in periodicals, on stage, in films and on numerous items of mass-marketed merchandise. Could Bonzo have been a Staffordshire Bull Terrier puppy?

"So glad You've Come"

This antiquarian postcard from the 1920s shows a little girl greeting her dog with a pawshake. Definitely a Hound!

A 1930s postcard by the popular British dog portrait artist, Fannie Moody (1861–1948), featuring two anthropomorphised Spaniels. In front of them lies a copy of *Our Dogs*, the oldest canine newspaper in the world, which began in 1895 and is still going strong today.

TWA BRAW LADS.

These 'twa braw lads' (Scots for 'two fine lads') from this 1930s postcard are – unsurprisingly – both Scotties. Originally known as the Aberdeen Terrier, the breed acquired the title Scottish Terrier in 1879 after its popularity had spread more widely.

If you don't write we'll be on your track.

This 1932 postcard features a row of Bloodhounds – a breed that was believed to be first developed by monks at the monastery of St Hubert in Belgium at the turn of the first millennium. In the nineteenth century, the original Chien de Saint-Hubert breed started to die out, but its Bloodhound descendants were used to rescue it from extinction.

CHAPTER 5

DOG DAYS

Previous spread: This promotional photo from May 1969, issued by a Berlin safety harness manufacturer, shows Waldi the Dachshund in his new belted contraption. As car culture progressed in the 1960s, so did motoring accessories for dogs.

This page: Two elegant Edwardian ladies play with a Cocker Spaniel and a skipping rope on the beach in this charming postcard.

A well-to-do couple and a pack of dogs including an English Setter, Irish Setter, Springer Spaniels and a Pekingese puppy (carried), *c.* 1910. The back of the photo bears the message 'From Mrs Marling'.

THE OLIVE BRANCH   C24.

An Edwardian studio photograph featuring an alert Collie looking off-camera. Photographers would often hide special treats in their pocket to get a dog to look their way for a portrait. The famous Victorian dog photographer Thomas Fall was said to keep some Spratt's biscuits in his coat pocket at all times.

Two young silent film actors pose with their Borzois. The sepia postcard dates from the early 1920s when all types of pedigrees were very much in fashion among the new celebrities and European royals alike. The Borzoi originated in sixteenth-century Russia by crossing Salukis and European sighthounds with thick-coated Russian breeds.

A 1920s hand-painted postcard showing the English actress and model Miss Gladys Cooper posing with a Scottish Deerhound. This ancient breed is a large rough-coated dog of the Greyhound type, originally known as the Scottish Wolfdog but later developed as a deer-coursing breed.

This press photo from the 1920s shows a champion German Shepherd Dog making a fine leap through a hoop in trials at Crystal Palace. Due to anti-German sentiment during the First World War, the breed was renamed the Alsatian, referring to the German–French border area of Alsace-Lorraine. The original name was reinstated in the 1970s.

A hand-painted artisan postcard from Paris, France, *c.* 1930s. French Bulldogs became popular in France after lace artisans moved from Nottingham to France in the 1860s, bringing their miniature Bulldogs with them. The breed – renamed the *Bouledogue Français* – became an instant Parisian sensation. The ruffled collar depicted here was a 'fashion' recreation of the stiff badger- or boar-hair collars worn as neck protection by the breed's fighting ancestors.

2092 Where's that Boatman?

A popular postcard from the 1930s showing a selection of Terrier types waiting to take to the waters. Cairn Terriers became even more in demand after the 1939 cinematic release of *The Wizard of Oz*, starring Toto the dog. Toto was actually Terry (a bitch), but her name was later permanently changed to Toto after the huge success of the film.

A press photo taken in London in the 1940s featuring a talented Flat-coated Retriever. This gundog breed became popular in the late 1800s on English shooting estates. The founder of The Kennel Club, Mr S. E. Shirley, who was its chairman from 1873 to 1899, was a great enthusiast of the breed.

Bertram Mills was once called the renovator of the British circus. His family-owned troupe travelled throughout the UK from the late 1880s. This press photo is from the early 1950s and features one of their most popular acts, 'Louise and her Dogs'. Circus dogs were a source of entertainment going back to Georgian times.

A snapshot of Miss Kate Ward, a.k.a. 'Camberley Kate'. Miss Ward was a well-known dog rescuer in Camberley, Surrey, in the 1950s. Every day, she and her pack of strays would make the four-mile round trip from her cottage to the town centre in order to collect donations and sell postcards to help pay for the dogs' upkeep. She never turned away a dog, taking in over 600 strays until her death in 1979.

A black and white promotional portrait showing three
beautiful Cocker Spaniels sitting in front of a NSU Prinz 1000,
manufactured in West Germany between 1963 and 1972.

A Crufts 1956 press photo of a Chihuahua (Smooth Coat) waiting to be taken into the show. The smallest breed in the world takes its name from the Mexican state where it became fashionable in the late nineteenth century. From there its popularity spread to America, where its association with celebrity owners made it famous worldwide.

A promotional postcard advertising Black & White Scotch whisky, *c.* late 1980s. The story goes that the Victorian whisky baron James Buchanan had visited a dog show where he was inspired to use two Terriers as mascots for the brand: one black (a Scottie) and one white (a Westie).

CHAPTER 6
HOUNDS OF WAR

3rd Battn Grenadiers Pet Dog "Modder." Brought by the Regiment from the battlefield.

Previous spread: A First World War cabinet card featuring an Imperial Germany Army officer with his dog, a Shepherd Collie breed type. The photograph was taken by C. F. Paul from Colmar, France, a small town near the border with Germany.

This page: An antiquarian colourised postcard (*c.* early 1900s) of 'Private Modder', a farm Collie who earned Queen Victoria's South Africa Medal with six clasps and the King's South Africa Medal with two clasps serving the King's 3rd Grenadier Guards in the Boer War. This famous dog was found with her pups at the Battle of Modder River on 28 November 1899. She became the regiment's mascot, and her image was later commercialised in postcard form.

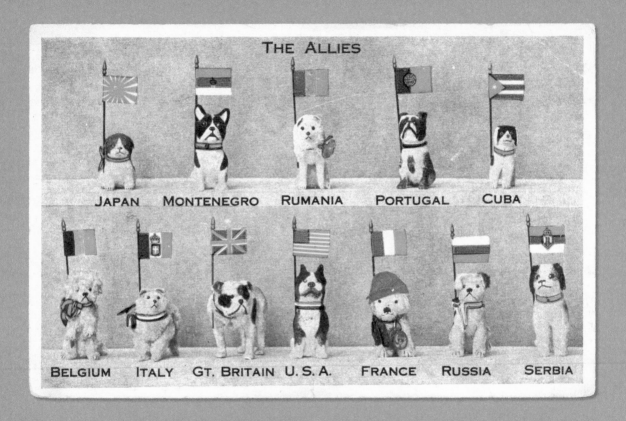

A very popular postcard from the First World War representing the major Allied powers. Proceeds from its sales went to Allied relief efforts.

"A SCRAP OF PAPER"

This Allied propaganda postcard from the First World War refers to the Convention of 1839 – the 'scrap of paper' – which upheld Belgium's independence and neutrality. Germany's breach of this treaty triggered the start of the war in 1914.

Le Chien sanitaire ... et patriote !

Déposé, reproduction interdite.

A humorous First World War postcard showing a Red Cross dog holding a French cap in its mouth and urinating on a German soldier's helmet. This was one of the most popular postcards of this period.

French First World War soldiers pose for the camera with their dog. 'Gas dogs' did vital work during the war, alerting soldiers to incoming mustard gas and helping to search for the wounded. It is estimated that over one million dogs died during the hostilities.

DAYS OF THE GREAT WAR.

George Chapman,
PHOTOGRAPHER.
63 STATION ROAD,
BEXHILL-ON-SEA.

Postcard of British First World War Royal Artillery soldiers and their mascot, an Irish Terrier. Terriers were often trained as guard dogs, as well as being used to carry messages between the trenches – a critical role in an age before widespread electronic communication.

An album photograph of a British First World War soldier in tropical kit and his Terrier. Many soldiers had portrait photos taken with their dogs before they went to war.

A personal photograph taken from a photo album, date unknown, showing a naval commander holding up a Bearded Collie type breed. For many years dogs were considered lucky mascots of the Royal Navy, often undertaking extraordinary journeys at sea until the practice was banned in 1975.

36

Dogs with first-aid and stimulants off to search
for wounded in inaccessible parts of no-mans-land

Stereoview card showing dog handlers from the Royal
Engineers Signal Service. Dogs loaded with first-aid
packs were used to search out wounded soldiers in the
inaccessible parts of no-man's land.

BOYS FROM RIPON.

This First World War postcard shows a troop of British soldiers from the West Yorkshire Regiment with their small Spitz type mascot. Ripon in North Yorkshire was the location of a vast training camp during the war, accommodating 30,000 troops.

A Bosche sniper worries the Seaforths who are
snatching an hour's respite with their mascot

Stereoview card, *c.* 1915. Seaforth Highlanders in the
trenches have a moment of respite from snipers with
their mascot dog resting by their feet.

CAPTURED AT COURCELETTE

Canadian Official

A photogravure postcard printed in Great Britain by the Pictorial Newspaper Co. (1918), featuring a Canadian officer holding a Terrier in front of a wall of sandbags. The caption 'Captured at Courcelette' refers to a commune in the Somme department of northern France, which suffered some of the heaviest battle tolls of the First World War.

Album photograph showing a little Dachshund cross peering out of a German officer's car. From his insignia it seems he was a Luftwaffe (German Air Force) Oberfeldwebel, which was a senior NCO rank. The photo is dated 20 September 1939, less than three weeks after the outbreak of the Second World War.

A Royal Artillery group photo from the Second World War with their mascot dog pictured in the middle. The back of the photo bears the message: 'To Mr Smith, with all our thanks and very best wishes for Xmas and the New Year from the No. 6 Anti-Tank Range Det [Detachment] RA, Dec 1943.'

CHAPTER 7

SHOWTIME

Previous spread: A Wire Fox Terrier named Torkard Susan and his dapper owner, Mr A. Francis, at Crufts 1952. Back then the show environment was quite basic with wooden folding tables and sawdust on the floor. However, the exhibitors came dressed in their best hats, ties and sometimes fur coats.

This page: A photogravure (a combination of photograph and engraving) of Dandy, a Gordon Setter. He is known to be the winner of the first formal dog show, which took place in Newcastle-upon-Tyne in 1859, making this one of the rarest photographic items in The Kennel Club collections.

An Edwardian postcard (*c.* 1900s), depicting well-heeled ladies showing their dogs at Burnham and Bourne End Dog Show. The mixed class of breeds being shown includes a Pug, King Charles Spaniel, Poodle, Shepherd breed type and Old English Sheepdog.

CHAMPION POODLE, "THE PILOT".

The Pilot, a black Standard Poodle owned by Mrs B. Parker, and winner of Best of Breed at Crufts in 1900 and 1901. This postcard (*c.* 1918, printed in Bavaria) shows the champion with a dashing bow holding up his topknot.

4731. BORZOIS. - JUDGES LTD

An Edwardian postcard (*c.* 1920s) showing three Borzois at an outdoor dog show. One of the dogs is putting in a good yoga stretch before the start of the competition.

An exhibitor with her two Old English Sheepdogs at The Kennel Club show, 1922, held at the Crystal Palace in south London. Cat and dog shows had been staged here since the 1870s. The original Crystal Palace building was commissioned for the Great Exhibition of 1851 in Hyde Park, London, and was relocated to south London the following year. Sadly, the famous Crystal Palace burned down in a devastating fire on 30 November 1936.

An Irish Red and White Setter (currently one of our vulnerable native breeds) and his handler get papped by press photographers at Crufts 1933. This photo is from *Hutchinson's Popular & Illustrated Dog Encyclopaedia*, one of the many rare books held in The Kennel Club library.

A West Highland White Terrier being judged at the National Terrier Championship show at Olympia in 1947. The judge, Mrs Winant, arrived from the US on the *Queen Elizabeth* transatlantic liner, landing only the day before the show.

Crufts 1948 Best in Show winner, a Cocker Spaniel named Tracy Witch of Ware, and his owner on the right, Mr H. S. Lloyd. The Keddell Memorial Trophy on the left was named for Robert Keddell, Crufts' show manager from 1894 to 1924. The lady in the hat is Mrs Emma Cruft (Charles's wife), who took over the show after her husband's death in 1938, selling it to The Kennel Club four years later.

A press photo of competitors heading to Olympia for Crufts 1950. Miss A. Goodman of Romford carries one Pekingese, Shan of Shah, in a basket and holds the other – Wee of the Wisp – under her arm.

Well-dressed men in suits and ties get their dogs ready for inspection at the Welsh Terrier judging in the Grand Hall at Olympia, London, 1950.

This press photo from Crufts 1950 captures Miss E. Snelling of Reading with her beautiful Afghan Hounds entering the show. Notice the bystanders in the background staring at the scene as if they had just seen a glamorous movie star.

An Elk Hound, Fourwents Carlo, is photographed by the press after winning Best of Breed at Crufts 1950. Photographers have always been an integral part of Crufts, often having to act quickly to capture the dog looking its best.

A press photo from Crufts 1950, showing a proud exhibitor holding his Pomeranian. The Pomeranian breed was first seen in the UK in 1870 and became a great favourite of Queen Victoria, whose dogs were frequently exhibited in London.

An original press photo from Crufts 1951, held in Olympia, London. Pekingese were first introduced to Britain through a little dog named Looty (or Lootie), aptly named after she was acquired by Captain John Hart Dunne during the looting of the Old Summer Palace near Beijing, China, in 1860. Captain Dunne presented the dog to Queen Victoria to add to her royal collection.

Mrs D. Metten of Kenton, one of the first arrivals at the 1953 show with her two Afghan Hounds, Sinndi of Carloway (left) and Midas of Khorrassan (right). Afghan Hounds are a popular attraction on Hound Day at Crufts as photographers are always drawn to their long and flowing hair.

A black and white press photo showing a general view of the first day at Crufts 1953, with Terrier judging in progress. On the far left are Bedlingtons, in the centre Cairn Terriers and on the right Scottish Terriers.

This press photo taken at Crufts 1953 in London's Olympia features seven-year-old Valerie Rowley using her mother's St Bernard, Daphne of Coplaydean, as a backrest while she sketches. In 1985, The Kennel Club established The Young Kennel Club (YKC) for young dog show enthusiasts, providing opportunities for children to connect with like-minded individuals and bond with their own canine companions.

A press photo featuring Tzigane Aggri of Nashend, a Standard Poodle owned by Mrs A. Proctor, Best in Show at Crufts 1955. The trophy displayed in the photo was originally awarded to Sir Malcolm Campbell for breaking the land speed record in 1928. However, Lady Dorothy Campbell, Sir Malcolm's ex-wife and a breeder of Poodles, donated it to The Kennel Club in 1951 after his death.

A non-cooperative Best in Show winner! Receiving the trophy is Volkrijk of Vorden and his owner Mrs Rene Tucker. This year – 1957 – was the first and so far only time the Best in Show at Crufts has been won by a Keeshond, a Spitz type breed originating from the Netherlands. It is often nicknamed the 'Dutch Barge Dog'.

After travelling all night from his home in Bradford, Yorkshire, Mr P. Wheeler snatches forty winks with his two Kerry Blue Terriers at Crufts 1959.

Great Danes, large dogs with big hearts, are hard to miss at Crufts on the day of the Working Group. This press photo from Crufts 1966 shows a Great Dane named Sawpitsville with owner Mr J. Ellyatt. Here Sawpitsville takes a gentle interest in one-year-old Sarah Needham, who is carried on her father's back.

This little champ is an English Toy Terrier, Stealaway Golden Girl, winner of the Toy Group at Crufts 1970. She is being congratulated by Princess Margaretha of Sweden. Sadly, English Toy Terriers, once so popular in the early twentieth century, are now one of The Kennel Club's vulnerable native breeds.

Mrs Valerie Foss judging English Setters at Windsor Championship Dog Show, 1970. On the left is Show Champion Monksriding Ernford Flamingo, and on the right is Show Champion Hurwyn Morning Glory. The photo was taken by C. M. Cooke and Son. As a judge Mrs Foss was mainly involved with gundogs, judging Best in Show at Crufts in 2010.

Who is sleepier: the child or the Pointer? Photographed on Gundog Day at Crufts 1970, this little girl is sound asleep on her dog after a long day of showing.

Copyright © 2024 The Kennel Club

The right of The Kennel Club to be identified as the Author of
the Work has been asserted by it in accordance with the
Copyright, Designs and Patents Act 1988.

First published in 2024 by
WILDFIRE
an imprint of HEADLINE PUBLISHING GROUP

1

Cataloguing in Publication Data is available from the British Library

Hardback ISBN 978-1-0354-0969-3

Design by Amazing15
Consultant editor Heidi Hudson MA

Printed and bound in Italy by L.E.G.O. S.p.A.

MIX
Paper | Supporting
responsible forestry
FSC® C104740

Headline's policy is to use papers that are natural, renewable and recyclable products and made from
wood grown in well-managed forests and other controlled sources. The logging and manufacturing
processes are expected to conform to the environmental regulations of the country of origin.

HEADLINE PUBLISHING GROUP
An Hachette UK Company
Carmelite House
50 Victoria Embankment
London EC4Y 0DZ

www.headline.co.uk
www.hachette.co.uk